Note to Educators and Parents

Reading is such an exciting adventure for young children! They are beginning to integrate their oral language skills with written language. To encourage children along the path to early literacy, books must be colorful, engaging, and interesting; they should invite the young reader to explore both the print and the pictures.

Animals I See at the Zoo is a new series designed to help children read about twelve fascinating animals. In each book, young readers will learn interesting facts about the featured animal.

Each book is specially designed to support the young reader in the reading process. The familiar topics are appealing to young children and invite them to read — and re-read — again and again. The full-color photographs and enhanced text further support the student during the reading process.

In addition to serving as wonderful picture books in schools, libraries, homes, and other places where children learn to love reading, these books are specifically intended to be read within an instructional guided reading group. This small group setting allows beginning readers to work with a fluent adult model as they make meaning from the text. After children develop fluency with the text and content, the book can be read independently. Children and adults alike will find these books supportive, engaging, and fun!

— Susan Nations, M.Ed., author, literacy coach,
and consultant in literacy development

I like to go to
the zoo. I see
monkeys at
the zoo.

5

"Ooh, eek," monkeys whoop and shriek. It is fun to watch them play.

Monkeys have hands and feet like ours. They. hold on to things with their hands and feet.

Monkeys swing on vines. They climb up in the trees.

Some monkeys look for food in the trees. They may eat leaves, flowers, insects, or fruit.

Some monkeys live in the trees. Some monkeys live on the ground.

Some monkeys
are small
and furry.

Some monkeys
are large
and fierce.

18

Some monkeys
are large
and fierce.

I like to see monkeys at the zoo. Do you?

Glossary

fierce — wild, cruel

shriek — to cry out in a loud, piercing way

vines — plants with long, thin stems

For More Information

Books

Arnold, Caroline. *Monkey*. New York: Morrow Junior Books, 1993.

Greenwood, Elinor. *Rain Forest*. New York: DK Publishing, 2001.

Shahan, Sherry. *Feeding Time at the Zoo*. New York: Random House, 2000.

Web Sites

Chaffee Zoo

www.chaffeezoo.org/zoo/animals/colobus.html
For a photo and facts about the colobus monkey
www.chaffeezoo.org/zoo/animals/macaque.html
For a photo and facts about the lion-tailed macaque

exZOOberance.com

www.exzooberance.com/virtual%20zoo/they%20walk/
monkey/monkey.htm
For monkey photos and facts

Index

feet, 8

flowers, 12

food, 12

fruit, 12

ground, 14

hands, 8

insects, 12

leaves, 12

play, 6

trees, 10, 12, 14

vines, 10

zoo, 4, 20

About the Author

JoAnn Early Macken is the author of a rhyming picture book, *Cats on Judy*, and *Animal Worlds*, a series of nonfiction picture books about animals and their habitats. Her poems have been published or accepted by *Ladybug*, *Spider*, *Highlights for Children*, and an anthology, *Stories from Where We Live: The Great Lakes*. A winner of the Barbara Juster Esbensen 2000 Poetry Teaching Award, she teaches poetry writing. She lives in Wisconsin with her husband and their two sons.